SURFING
HAWAII

Copyright 1972 By Allan Banker Wright Jr.

Copyright © Allan Banker Wright, Jr **1985**

Published and manufactured in the United States of America

Mountain & Sea Publishing
P.O. Box 126
Redondo Beach, CA. 90277

This book is printed on recycled paper.
No trees were cut down to make this paper!

"Take care of the earth and it will take care of you"

Mountain & Sea Book

This book . . . .
    is for the surfer . . .
    that he may know
    and enjoy
    the best of the Hawaiian Islands;
    that he may answer his every need,
    foster good nature
    by wave
    and in deed.

This book . . . .
    is for the surfer . . .
    that he may appreciate the best
    of his natural environment
    through caring
    and sharing . . .

              This book . . . .
                  is for the surfer . . .
                  that he may have at hand
                  a guide to new adventures
                  waiting waves
                  virgin beaches;
                  that whatever the season,
                  whatever the swell,
                  he may choose it well.

SAVE OUR SURF

Save Our Surf is a youthful movement made up of teenage surfers and other groups interested in preserving the natural surfing reefs from construction of hotels, breakwaters and boat harbors.

S.O.S. considers four outside forces as present dangers to Hawaiian surf.

1. CONSTRUCTION

2. POLLUTION

3. DENIAL OF ACCESS

4. OVERCROWDING

The first three are the direct results of **other** people against which the S.O.S. can initiate action. The fourth, overcrowding, results from the urbanizations of cities, people crowding into smaller and smaller areas while underpopulation exists in the outlying areas.

How can a handful of surfers stop a system seemingly bent on destroying the sport of surfing? **It's not easy.** Hours of hard work, research, and peaceful demonstrations have given S.O.S. a long record of achievement.

To insure victory, the **collective** support of all people who love the sea and want it to be the same tomorrow as it is today is desperately needed.

Whether you live in Hawaii or on the mainland lend a hand and support the cause. Preserve the environment as nature intended.

The Author . . .

CONTENTS

MAPS

To understand how to read maps,
these facts should be remembered:

1. Map sections progress **counter clock-wise** around each island.

2. Map pages read from **top to bottom.**

3. The shaded areas of the small maps refer to the shorelines of the large maps.

SEASONS

SUMMER

The summer swells begin to break along the south shore around the middle of April. Sizes average 2-5 feet with numerous 6-10 foot swells. By the end of September the swells are infrequent but occasional waves will break in October. Summer surf is generally smaller, less frequent and not nearly as strong as the big swells of Winter.

FALL

The months of September through November are the first to feel the powerful swells of Winter. Wave size shows a continual increase as the storms in the northern Pacific become stronger and more frequent. The shape of the surf is nearly perfect. Over the calm summer months, the sands have had time to settle along the reefs leaving a contoured bottom over which waves breaks with machine-like precision.

WINTER

The biggest waves of the year break between December and February. Oftentimes the northern shores will close out, with the waves breaking all at once. During these times only 1 or 2 spots will be surfable.

Heavy rains and kona wind frequently produce unridable conditions. Churning whitewater also causes a shifting of bottom sand which produces an erratic breaking pattern.

SPRING

Between March and June, the winter swells show a steady decrease in both size and frequency. Although large waves still break, they come and go quickly, lasting only one or two days.

The spring surf is usually well-shaped. As the number of storms decrease, the sands have a chance to settle, helping produce the clean lines found during this period.

WINDS

There are two basic types of wind that affect Hawaiian waves, tradewinds and kona winds. Both play important roles in determining the quality or shape of the surf.

TRADEWIND

95% of the wind that strikes the islands originates in the northeast and is commonly referred to as "tradewind" or the "prevailing trades". The trades have various effects upon the shorelines.

Along the **north, south** and **west** shores, the trades produce ideal offshore or sidewind effects upon the surf. But on the **eastern** coast the trades blow directly onshore creating bumpy surface conditions most of the year.

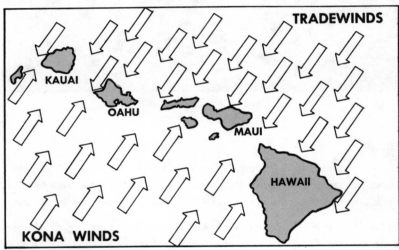

KONA WIND

Occasionally, storms from the south Pacific send winds onto Hawaiian shores. These warm breezes are referred to as KONA (south) WIND.

Kona winds produce the opposite effects of the tradewinds. During kona conditions, the **north, south** and **west** will experience onshore breezes. The ocean's surface will be choppy, unfavorable for surfing. On the **east** shore, perfect offshore conditions will prevail. The surf spots that are blownout will be glassy smooth.

Note: The above conditions generally hold true for all islands. Geographical position and local hill formations can produce slight variations.

One of the most important influences on surfing is the direction from which the ocean swells arrive. This point of origin determines the side of the island which will receive the surf and which area will have the best shape.

WINTER swells are born from fierce storms in the **north** and **west** Pacific. These powerful swells generate strong surf along the NORTH, WEST, and EASTERN shorelines.

During the summer months, waves are generated from storms located in the south Pacific where Winter is in full force. These warm, blue swells will cause surf along any shoreline with a southerly exposure. South swells have no effect upon the northern coasts.

Note: Although swells can produce surf along many breaks, some spots will have better quality than others. This is a result of the different positions reefs have in relation to incoming swells.

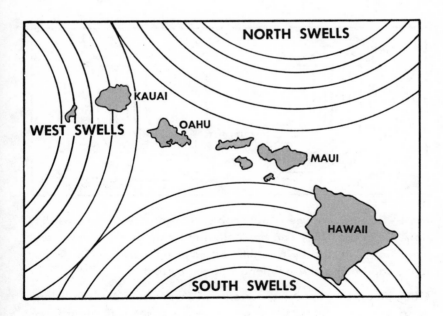

CURRENTS

The main difference between the surf on the mainland and in Hawaii is the power generated by the breaking wave. The forces created are much greater, mainly because the islands lack a continental shelf to slow down the swell. Nothing but a coral reef stands between the fast-moving, ocean swell and the sandy shoreline.

The most dangerous threat for the swimmer or surfer, especially the inexperienced, is being caught in a powerful current. Various types of these ocean currents are responsible for 80% of the drownings and near drownings in Hawaii. The following will help you to understand the form which a current can take.

RIP-CURRENTS

Rip-currents are created when large volumes of water flow into shallow areas near shore. The force of the water causes strong surface currents to flow back to sea, along the quickest and easiest route they can find (see diagram).

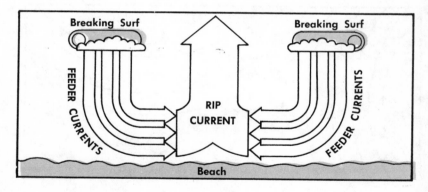

These currents produce a noticeable chop on the surface as they flow out to sea. They can be spotted not only by the water's seaward flow, but also by a slightly off-color appearance. This is due to the sand being carried along with the current.

Often-times, two opposing currents will meet near the shore, creating one powerful rip which will move out to sea with great force.

BACKWASH

A backwash is a current formed after a large wave has swept up a steep beach and is returning to sea. The slope of the beach causes the returning water to increase in speed as it flows back to sea. When the "backwash" current meets the incoming swell, a bumpy and unpredictable condition will result. This spot usually marks the end of the line for the wave rider.

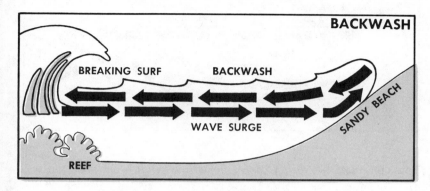

INSHORE CHANNELS AND HOLES

At some beaches, strong currents create channels or holes in the sand bottom. After a wave has swept up the beach, it will return faster and with greater force at the point where it flows into one of these channels or holes. This kind of current creates a strong underwater flow and is very difficult to detect.

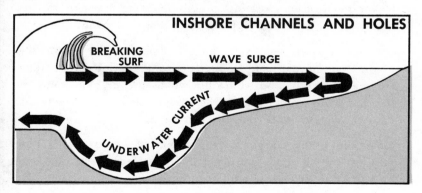

UNDERTOW

Undertows and rips are often confused. The main thing to remember is that a rip is primarily a surface current, while an undertow sweeps back from the shore under the water's surface.

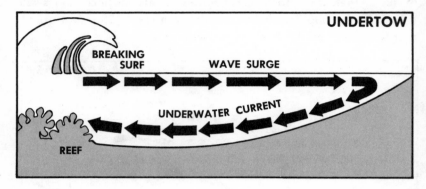

You can feel the effect of an undertow when you are standing or swimming near shore. There is a strong sucking motion of the water as it flows back and out to sea. These "suck-backs" are especially dangerous for the unwary. If the sand bank collapses, you may be caught in a strong undercurrent and be swept to sea.

RULES TO REMEMBER

1. **Never** swim directly against a current. Some move as fast as five miles an hour and fighting them will only exhaust you.

2. The best way to escape a rip-current is to swim diagonally across the current until you come to the edge of it. Then continue into the area where the waves are breaking and let the surf carry you back to the beach. If you stay with the current, you may find yourself miles out to sea.

   However, if the current is very strong, it would be wiser to relax and let it carry you along until it's force dissapates and then you can make your way back to shore.

3. The important thing to remember is that you must have an **understanding** of the currents prior to entering the water. Remember, there is no rule — each area is different and will have its own special problems.

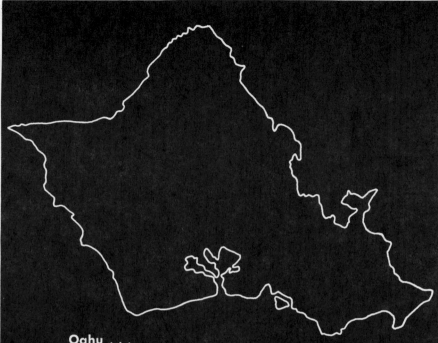

Oahu . . .
> the gathering place,
> where the waves of the world
> get together;
> where an endless summer sun
> decorates the weather;
>
> crossroads of the surfing set,
> where every type of wave
> lures the best,
> and man is put to the ultimate test;
> where fifty foot waves
> intrigue the mind,
> the greatest sensation the surfer will find;
>
> where honolulu and waikiki
> high rise to the sky,
> and cause a little tear to form
> in every surfers eye;
> where beauty . . . yet remains
> 'tho sadly suffers
>   growing pains.

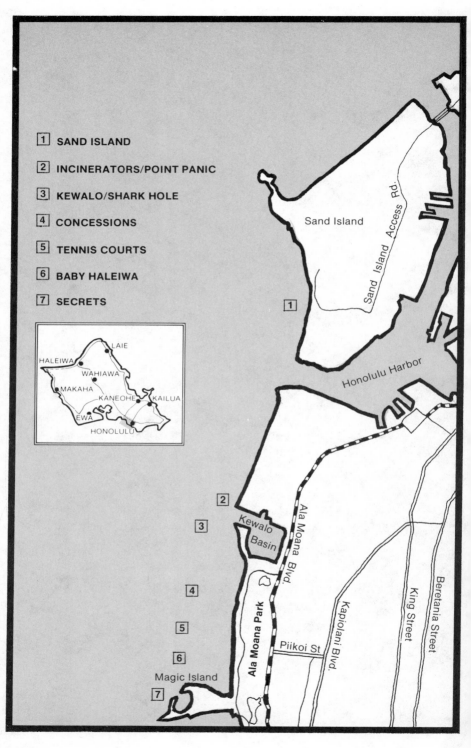

1 **SAND ISLAND**

2 **INCINERATORS/POINT PANIC**

3 **KEWALO/SHARK HOLE**

4 **CONCESSIONS**

5 **TENNIS COURTS**

6 **BABY HALEIWA**

7 **SECRETS**

14

Total involvement in a clean Hawaiian tube.

Shoreline: This is a portion of Oahu's famous South Shore. The outer reefs produce clean, warm tubes during summer months. On shore, parks and sandy beaches offer unlimited recreational facilities.

Wind: Constant offshore trades produce ideal year 'round surfing conditions. Kona storms produce bumpy and uneven swells.

Swell: Consistent 2 to 5 foot surf with occasional 6 to 10 foot days pour onto this coast. West swells will sometimes produce unexpected winter surf.

Notes: Rocks and coral heads are found on the reefs — avoid stepping into unknown depths. . . . Between Sand Island and Kewalo Basin, deep water and sewage attract sharks.

SURFING AREAS

SAND ISLAND
Various reef breaks. Peaks and lines. Usually uncrowded. Sewage and sharks. Summer surf.

INCINERATORS/POINT PANIC
Fabulous bodysurfing. Fast tubular rights. Breaks into seawall. Summer.

SHARK HOLE
Peak lefts into channel. Perfection tubes. Strong currents. Needs a south, summer swell.

CONCESSIONS
Short but hollow tubes. Right and left. Needs a 2-6 foot south swell.

TENNIS COURTS
Long, powerful rights. Thick peak lefts. 2-10 feet. Crowded summer spot.

BABY HALEIWA
Needs 5 feet to work. Peak take-off. Long right, thick, short left. Summer.

SECRETS
Long, heavy lefts. Outside of Magic Island breakwall. Usually uncrowded. Summertime power.

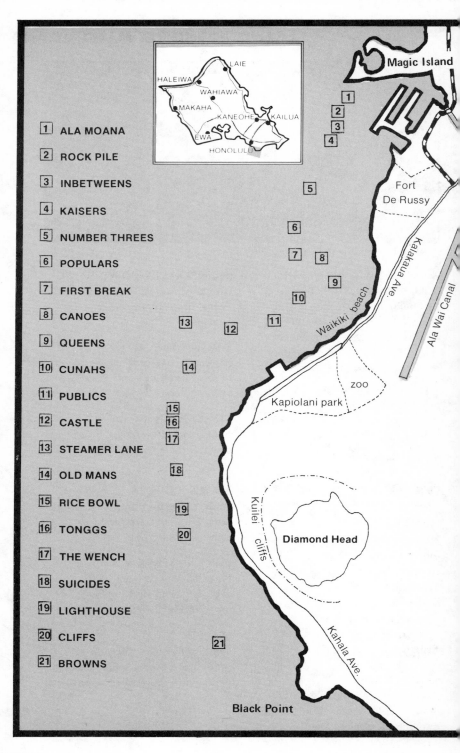

1 ALA MOANA

2 ROCK PILE

3 INBETWEENS

4 KAISERS

5 NUMBER THREES

6 POPULARS

7 FIRST BREAK

8 CANOES

9 QUEENS

10 CUNAHS

11 PUBLICS

12 CASTLE

13 STEAMER LANE

14 OLD MANS

15 RICE BOWL

16 TONGGS

17 THE WENCH

18 SUICIDES

19 LIGHTHOUSE

20 CLIFFS

21 BROWNS

Magic Island

Fort De Russy

Kalakaua Ave.

Ala Wai Canal

Waikiki beach

ZOO

Kapiolani park

Kuilei cliffs

Diamond Head

Kahala Ave.

Black Point

HALEIWA LAIE
WAHIAWA
MAKAHA
KANEOHE KAILUA
EWA
HONOLULU

Shoreline: This is the fabulous South Shore of Oahu. Over its reefs are found the best summer waves in the world. All types can be ridden . . . from the thick lefts of "Publics" to the thin, smoking tubes of "Ala Moana". Narrow trails lead down the Diamond Head cliffs to the reef breaks below. . . . Private beachfront restricts access to the reefs off Black Point.

Wind: Waikiki is blessed with constant offshore winds. . . Gusty trades blast the coast between Diamond Head and Black Point. Kona storms bring irregular and choppy seas to this entire shoreline.

Swell: South swells produce 2 to 4 foot surf with occasional 6 to 10 foot days. . . . Ocean swells pound Diamond Head and Black Point year 'round.

Notes: South shore surfing areas are usually very crowded.

SURFING AREAS

ALA MOANA
Churning left tube. 2-12 feet, south swell. Wicked inside bowl. Deep channel. Crowded summer spot.

ROCK PILE
Hollow peaks, right and left. Shallow coral reef. Summer tubes.

INBETWEENS
Fast right meeting Kaisers left. Mushy. Needs 5-8 foot south swell.

KAISERS
Long, hollow lefts and short tubular rights. 3-8 foot south swell. Deep channel. Summer madness.

NUMBER THREES
Perfection right tubes. 3-10 feet. South swell. Paddling channel. Summertime.

High and tight at "Kaiser's Bowl" — south shore, Oahu.

POPULARS
Thick rights over deep reef. Works above 5 feet, south swell. Crowded summer spot.

FIRST BREAK
Easy rights and lefts. Needs size to break. Outside Canoes. Strong summer surf.

CANOES
Gentle lefts and rights. Very crowded with tourist and canoes. A popular summer spot.

QUEENS
Clean rights off small peak. Works any size south swell. Offshore winds. A very popular summer area.

CUNAHS
Large mellow lefts. Needs 5 feet or better before it shows. Deep water reef. Summertime!

PUBLICS
Long, milky lefts. 1-12 feet, south swell. Coral heads on inside reef. Located in front of War Natatorium.

CASTLES
Mile-long lefts during huge swell. Coral reef inside. No channel. Summer surf.

STEAMER LANE
Giant 30 foot lefts. Endless rides. Very rarely breaks.

In the lip at "Ala Moana" — south shore, Oahu.

A peaceful campsite overlooking surf break — leeward, Oahu.

Kneeboarder slashes toward the shoulder as the hook smokes overhead.

Water level view as wave and rider churn toward the channel.

OLD MAN'S
Soft rights and lefts. 2-10 foot, south swell. Paddling channel. Fronts Canoe Club.

RICEBOWL
Smoking rights. Shallow reef, best at high tide. Needs 3-10 foot summer swell.

TONGGS
Peak lefts, fast and hollow. 1-8 feet. South swell. Channel. Summer surf.

THE WENCH
Short, right sliders. Breaks from 2-5 feet, south swell. Private property hampers access.

SUICIDES
3-10 foot lefts. Usually bumpy. Hard to reach. Summer only.

LIGHTHOUSE
Steep, right peaks with hollow inside line-up. Usually 2 feet bigger than other spots. Offers summer and winter juice.

CLIFFS
Various reef breaks. Peaks and lines. Surfable the year 'round.

BROWNS
Big wave spot of the south shore. Crushing rights breaking ½ mile out. Dangerous reefs and currents inside. Experts only. Works both summer and winter.

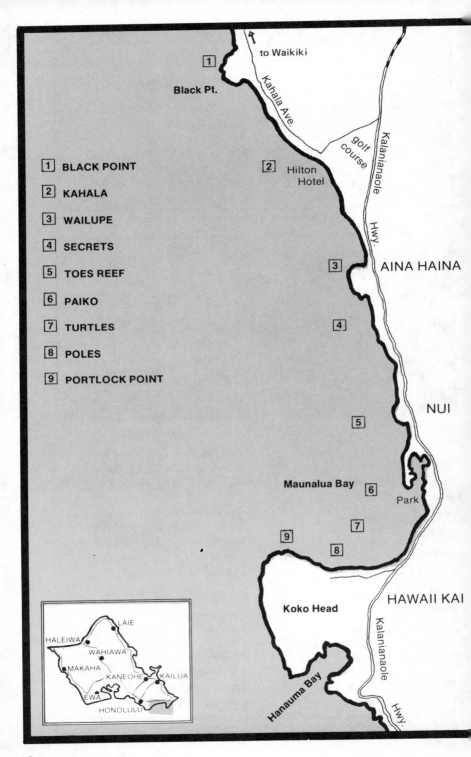

1 BLACK POINT

2 KAHALA

3 WAILUPE

4 SECRETS

5 TOES REEF

6 PAIKO

7 TURTLES

8 POLES

9 PORTLOCK POINT

Shoreline: Private beachfront homes hamper access to the coastal surfing areas. A few scattered parks provide entry but long walks or paddles are needed to reach the outer breaks.

Wind: Early mornings or late evenings are best. By mid-morning, howling trades have usually whipped the seas into unridable chop.

Swell: The south swells produce high quality summer tubes. West swells will sometimes bring small winter surf. The big northern swells fail to reach this shore.

Notes: Coral heads and jagged rocks lurk below the surface. Use caution while surfing at low tide. . . . Wind and swell direction are very critical to the areas along this coast.

Carving into the whitewater.

SURFING AREAS

BLACK POINT
Various reef breaks. Rights and lefts. Body and board surfing. Has good size year 'round.

KAHALA
Perfection tubes. 2-6 feet, south swell. Usually windy. Summertime.

WAILUPE
Short but fast lefts. Breaks on outer reef. 2-6 feet, south swell.

SECRETS
Uncrowded lefts. Best with light winds. Hard to find! Best during Summer.

TOES REEF
Tubular rights and lefts when wind is calm. Private beachfront. Summer tubes.

PAIKO
Thin left off outer reef. 2-6 feet, south swell. Best at high tide. Summer.

TURTLES
Rights and lefts on outer reef. Fronts Maunalua Beach Park. Warm summer juice.

POLES
Quick lefts and rights. Inside point. 1-5 feet, south swell. Very windy.

PORTLOCK POINT
Long, thick lefts off KoKo Head. Works above 5 feet. Very windy. Summer heavies.

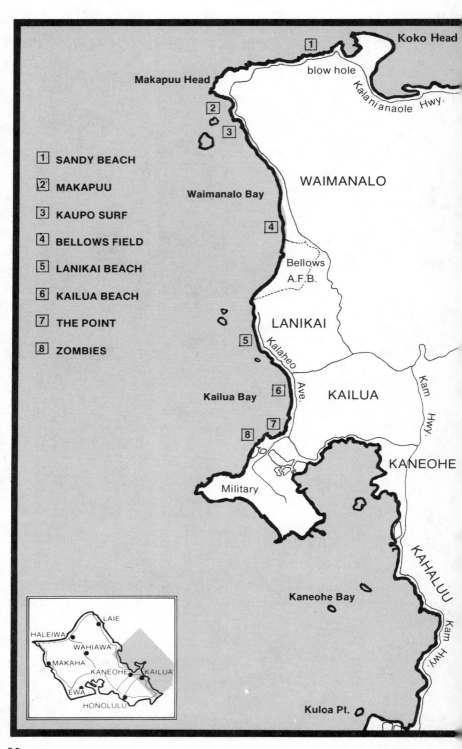

1 SANDY BEACH
2 MAKAPUU
3 KAUPO SURF
4 BELLOWS FIELD
5 LANIKAI BEACH
6 KAILUA BEACH
7 THE POINT
8 ZOMBIES

Koko Head

blow hole

Kalanianaole Hwy.

Makapuu Head

WAIMANALO

Waimanalo Bay

Bellows A.F.B.

LANIKAI

Kalaheo Ave.

KAILUA

Kailua Bay

Kam Hwy.

KANEOHE

Military

KAHALUU

Kam Hwy.

Kaneohe Bay

LAIE
HALEIWA
WAHIAWA
MAKAHA
KANEOHE   KAILUA
EWA
HONOLULU

Kuloa Pt.

KOKO HEAD TO MAKAPUU

Shoreline: The rugged cliffs of KokoHead gradually descend to the crushing shorebreak of Sandy Beach. Sharp lava fingers limit surfing to Sandy Beach.

Wind: Gusty trades produce unpredictable surface conditions. It can be smooth one minute and choppy the next.

Swell: Waves break year 'round. Shape is best during a strong **south swell.**

Notes: During strong surf, a rip-current flows between Sandy Beach and Haunama Bay . . . use caution before entering the water.

SURFING AREAS

SANDY BEACH
Popular bodysurfing area. Crushing shorebreak. Board surfing during big swells. Strong currents. Breaks year 'round.

MAKAPUU
Bodysurfing area. Peaks and walls. Sandy bottom. Breaks year 'round. Summer is best.

KAUPO SURF
Small beginners surf. Around point from Makapuu. Summer and Winter.

Slipping beneath the hook as rider inside scratches for safety.

Stacked to the horizon, north swells funnel onto the "Sunset" reef. Note . . . Absence of usual crowd.

MAKAPUU TO KANEHOE BAY

Shoreline: Parks and sandy beaches extend along this gentle eastern coast. Public right-a-ways are located where private property denies access. Protected lagoons offer safe swiming areas.

Wind: Strong onshore trades produce bumpy seas most of the year. Kona winds bring glassy surface conditions to this coast.

Swell: Thick, ocean swells create fabulous bodysurfing along the shores of Makapuu. . . . Between Waimanalo and Kailua, an outer reef quickly reduces ocean swells to shorebreak.

Notes: Due to pollution, swimming in Kanehoe Bay is not recommended. . . Kona wind and a strong swell bring fantastic surfing conditions.

BELLOWS FIELD

Small shorebreak waves. Good for beginners. Needs kona wind and big swell. Sandy bottom. Breaks year 'round.

LANIKAI BEACH

Small shorebreak tubes. Good beginners surf. Sandy bottom. Surfable Summer and Winter.

KAILUA BEACH

Small beginners surf. Sand bottom. Protected by outside reef. Summer and Winter.

THE POINT

Small lefts off lava point. Breaks 1-5 feet, any swell.

ZOMBIES

Small rights and lefts. On Gov't. property. Lava beach. Surfable year 'round.

The "Sunset" Lineup . . . Sunset Beach is a peak break followed by a long and powerful right slide. It requires a 6-foot winter swell to break and closes out near 18 feet. The take-off is almost straight up and down and breaks over a deep, jagged reef. The wave's shoulder eventually flattens into deep water. Depending on swell size and tide, a hollow section will sometimes develop, over the inside reef. Because of a shallow reef and inside section the lefts are rarely attempted. **Note:**

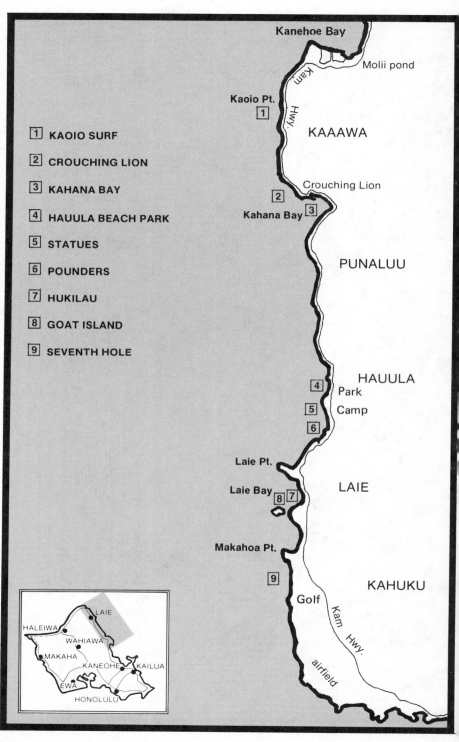

1 KAOIO SURF

2 CROUCHING LION

3 KAHANA BAY

4 HAUULA BEACH PARK

5 STATUES

6 POUNDERS

7 HUKILAU

8 GOAT ISLAND

9 SEVENTH HOLE

Kanehoe Bay

Molii pond

Kaoio Pt.

Kam. Hwy.

KAAAWA

Crouching Lion

Kahana Bay

PUNALUU

HAUULA

Park

Camp

Laie Pt.

Laie Bay

LAIE

Makahoa Pt.

KAHUKU

Golf

Kam. Hwy.

airfield

LAIE

HALEIWA

WAHIAWA

MAKAHA

KANEOHE

KAILUA

EWA

HONOLULU

Shoreline: White sandy beaches stretch for miles along this tropical windward coast. . . . A protective reef breaks up the ocean swells as they rush toward shore. . . . Along Kam highway, parks and public right-a-ways provide access to all surfing areas.

Wind: The prevailing trades blow onshore producing bumpy and uneven seas. Kona winds blow offshore and usually create flawless riding conditions.

Swell: Due to the outer reef, most areas have only small shorebreak waves. East wind swells produce gentle beginners surf during summer months.

Notes: Rapid currents flow along the outer reef — use caution while surfing unfamiliar breaks.

Bodysurfing—"Pounders Beach" windward, Oahu.

SURFING AREAS

KAOIO SURF
Gentle rights and lefts. Protected inside reef. Usually windy. Takes any swell. Summer and Winter.

CROUCHING LION
Long, crisp right. 2-10 feet. Best on strong swell and kona wind. Currents. Sharp coral reef. Experts only.

KAHANA BAY
Small beginners surf. 1-4 feet. Sandy bottom. Beach Park. Winter, any swell.

HAUULA BEACH PARK
Choppy, beginners surf. 1-4 feet. Best during the winter.

STATUES
2-6 foot rights and lefts. Needs kona wind. Located in front of CYO camp. Winter break.

POUNDERS
Bodysurfing break. Punishing shorebreak. Sandy bottom. Winter juice.

HUKILAU
Small, bumpy rights and lefts. Near Laie town. Best on east swell and kona wind.

GOAT ISLAND
Tubular left slides. Requires long walk or paddle. Uncrowded winter juice.

SEVENTH HOLE
Peaks, right and left. 2-8 feet, northeast swell, kona wind. Shallow reef. Wintertime.

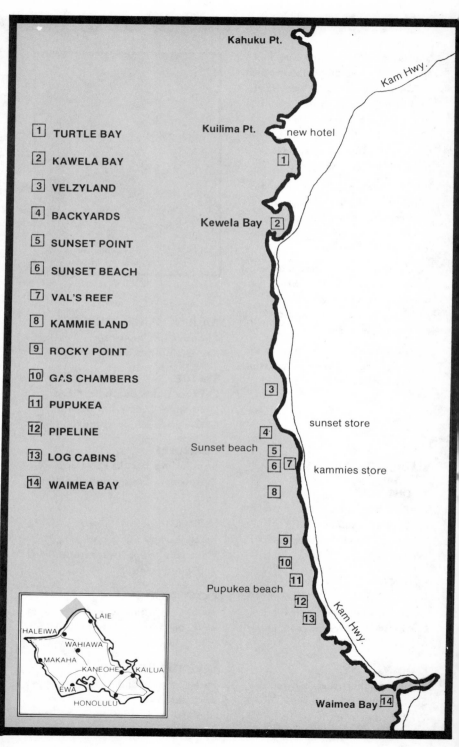

1 TURTLE BAY
2 KAWELA BAY
3 VELZYLAND
4 BACKYARDS
5 SUNSET POINT
6 SUNSET BEACH
7 VAL'S REEF
8 KAMMIE LAND
9 ROCKY POINT
10 GAS CHAMBERS
11 PUPUKEA
12 PIPELINE
13 LOG CABINS
14 WAIMEA BAY

Kahuku Pt.

Kam Hwy.

Kuilima Pt.   new hotel

Kewela Bay

sunset store

Sunset beach

kammies store

Pupukea beach

Kam Hwy.

Waimea Bay

LAIE
HALEIWA
WAHIAWA
MAKAHA
KANEOHE   KAILUA
EWA
HONOLULU

28

Shoreline: This is a portion of the famous North Shore of Oahu. Steep, high-powered waves can be ridden during winter months. Much of the oceanfront is private but parks and public right-a-ways allow easy access.

Wind: Prevailing sidewinds produce ideal conditions most of the year. Kona winds result in bumpy and unrideable seas.

Swell: Pumping north and west swells create unmatched winter perfection. Waves average 5 to 8 feet. 12 to 15 foot days are common. Two or three times a year titanic 18 to 30 foot surf hammers the shoreline.

Notes: During big surf, rip-currents develop near shore — use extreme caution before entering the water. . . . In cases of emergency, phones located near all surfing areas will bring immediate help.

SURFING AREAS

TURTLE BAY
Small beginners surf, 2-6 feet. Rights and lefts. Lava coast. Private beachfront. Winter.

KAWELA BAY
Point breaks, right and left. Sandy beach. Private property restricts access.

VELZYLAND
Top to bottom rights. Some lefts. Deep channel. Hazardous reef at low tide. Winter power!

BACKYARDS
Long, point rights. 2-8 feet, north or west swell. Wintertime.

SUNSET POINT
Strong rights off a shallow point. 3-10 feet, north or west swell. As the point closes, Sunset peak begins. Winter perfection.

"Sunset Beach" at its best . . . big and clean. North shore, Oahu.

SUNSET BEACH

Steep, shifting peak. Rights, few lefts. North or west swell. Strong rips and coral reef inside. The class spot of the North Shore.

VALS REEF

Inside reef of Sunset Beach. 2-5 feet. Rights and lefts. Coral shelf. Winter.

KAMMIELAND

Accross the channel from Sunset. Powerful rights and lefts. 5-12 feet, winter swell. Shallow reef. Strong inside currents.

ROCKY POINT

Various breaks along point. Rights and lefts. Peaks and lines. Breaks 3-10 feet, winter swell. Shallow reef runs to beach.

GAS CHAMBERS

Steep peaks over shallow reef. Tapering shoulder. Paddling channel. Takes any winter swell.

PUPUKEA

Powerful peaks, right or left. 3-10 foot, winter swell. Strong currents. Good bodysurfing. Sandy beach.

PIPELINE

Explosive **LEFT** tubes. Best on **west** swell. Shallow coral reef. Paddling channel.

Also, powerful **RIGHT** lines. Needs strong **north** swell. No channel. Strong currents. Coral reef. Winter juice.

LOG CABINS

Strong rights breaking over a shallow coral reef. Needs a 2-6 foot north or west swell. Down the beach from Pipeline. Winter.

WAIMEA BAY

15-30 foot peaks. Steep take-off followed by a mellowing shoulder. Works on a north or west swell. Thunderous shorebreak. Rip-currents. Experts only! !

A precision curl peels across the shallow "Pipeline" reef.

The "Sunset" Rip . . . Pictured is a hazardous condition which develops during times of large surf. It is known as a rip-current. The breaking surf (background) has created large amounts of energy which quickly take the form of a swift flowing current (seen in foreground). The current can be identified by its frothy and turbulent surface condition. **Note:** The surfer (lower left) is moving sideways 5-10 mph and faces a demanding paddle back to the break. See pages 12 and 32 for additional information.

SUNSET BEACH

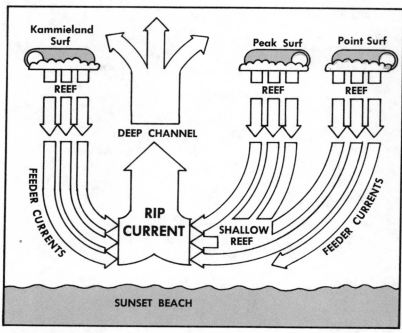

WAIMEA BAY

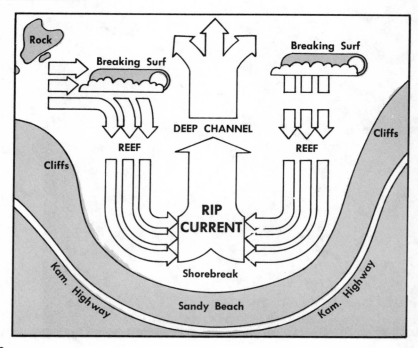

SUNSET AND WAIMEA RIP

During the winter months in Hawaii, giant waves pour onto the north shore of Oahu. Because of the surf's unusual size, most of the surfing areas close-out except for Sunset Beach and Waimea Bay.

Three or four times a year, 15-30 foot waves come thundering off the outside points of these well known areas. As walls of turbulent whitewater push shoreward, tremendous amounts of force are created. Some of this energy is expended on the sand as the water rushes up the beach, but large amounts flow down the shore seeking release. This escape is found in the form of a powerful rip-current flowing swiftly to sea.

The rip-currents of Sunset and Waimea are extremely dangerous and should never be taken lightly. An unwary swimmer or surfer can be swept to sea or caught in a murderous shorebreak in minutes. With an **understanding** of the natural forces at work, survival is possible.

PROCEDURE....

Being caught in the current is apparent if after a few minutes of swimming, no headway toward shore is being made. In fact, you are rapidly heading for the open sea. Once this situation is understood there are TWO courses of action:

1. Swim DIAGONALLY ACROSS the current and into the breaking whitewater.
2. RIDE WITH THE CURRENT until the flow dissipates. Then calmly swim into the whitewater.

Although these may be terrifying, the whitewater will provide a direct and swift journey to shore.

NEVER, under any circumstances swim toward the breaking waves on the LEFT side of Waimea Bay. This will result in a swift and final ride into the murderous shorebreak.

Remember, **UNDERSTAND THE SITUATION** before entering the water. If caught, **DON'T PANIC! !**

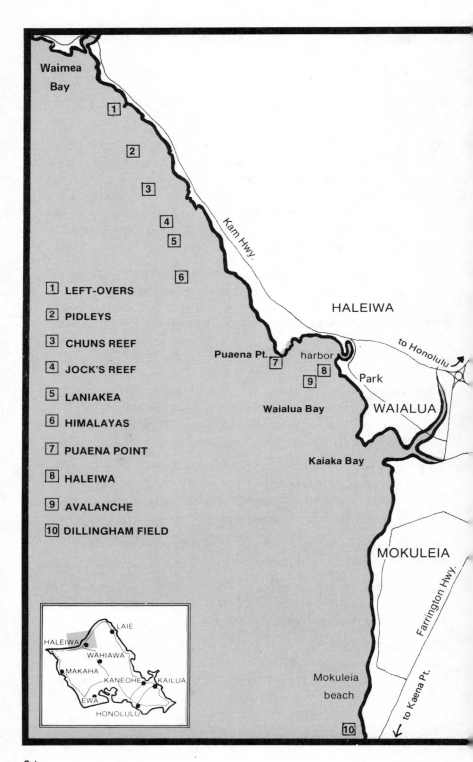

Waimea
Bay

1 LEFT-OVERS

2 PIDLEYS

3 CHUNS REEF

4 JOCK'S REEF

5 LANIAKEA

6 HIMALAYAS

7 PUAENA POINT

8 HALEIWA

9 AVALANCHE

10 DILLINGHAM FIELD

Kam Hwy.

HALEIWA

to Honolulu

Puaena Pt. 7 harbor 8

9 Park

Waialua Bay WAIALUA

Kaiaka Bay

MOKULEIA

Farrington Hwy.

Mokuleia
beach

to Kaena Pt.

10

LAIE

HALEIWA

WAHIAWA

MAKAHA

KANEOHE KAILUA

EWA

HONOLULU

A driving cutback as the shoulder suddenly flattens.

WAIMEA BAY TO MOKULEIA

Shoreline: Wide sandy beaches stretch for miles along this northern coast. . . . Countless point and reef breaks produce various types of winter surf. . . . Public parks and right-a-ways provide easy access to all areas.

Wind: The northeast trades produce ideal sidewinds nearly all year. Onshore kona winds quickly turn the surface to unrideable chop.

Swell: Potent north and west swells produce constant winter surf. Size, tide and swell direction determine which of the areas will work best. Summer swells fails to reach this coast.

Notes: Dangerous currents develop during strong surf — use extreme caution before entering the water.

SURFING AREAS

LEFT-OVERS
Left slides. 2-8 feet, north or west swell. In front of private property. Winter spot.

PIDLEYS
Long left or right. Winter swell. Uncrowded due to private property.

CHUNS REEF
Peak take-off followed by long tapering curl. Shallow reef inside. Lefts off point. Winter only.

JOCKS REEF
Pumping rights. Dangerous lava coast. Across channel from Lani-akea. Winter juice.

A smooth west swell peels over the outer "Haleiwa" reef — north shore, Oahu.

MOKULEIA TO KAENA POINT

Shoreline: The sandy beaches of Mokuleia gradually become the sharp lava of Kaena Point. . . . Channels in the outer reef provide dozens of unridden surf breaks.

Wind: Constant onshore breezes produce choppy seas. The occasional winds of a kona storm will create ideal surfing conditions.

Swell: North, east and west swells produce constant but sloppy surf. East wind swells can bring unexpected summer waves.

Notes: Coral and sharp rock lie beneath the surface — use caution when surfing at low tide.

SURFING AREAS

LANIAKEA

Long, right walls. Top to bottom in places. Flat spots. Best on north swell. Currents inside. Wintertime perfection.

HIMMALAYAS

Giant lefts, 3/4 miles out. 15-25 feet. Big and hairy. Strong currents. Experts only! !

PUAENA POINT

Excellent beginners area when small. Strong rights during big swell. Lava fingers! Winter.

HALEIWA

Critical right tubes. Softer lefts. 1-15 feet, north or west swell. Gentle surf when small. Dangerous currents during large surf. Winter only!

AVALANCHE

Terrifying lefts. 1 mile out. 10-25 feet. Hazardous reef. Strong currents. Rarely (if ever) ridden. Winter horror.

DILLINGHAM FIELD

Rights and lefts over outer reef. 2-10 feet. Coral reef. Best during kona winds and east swell. Winter.

"Early Country Morning" . . . A rare early morning view looking west from Waimea Bay to Kaena Point. The surf is real big. 18-20 foot swells can be seen pouring onto the north shore. The sea is smooth with only a slight offshore breeze, perfect conditions for riding big waves. **Note** . . . a strange haze lurking near Kaena Point.

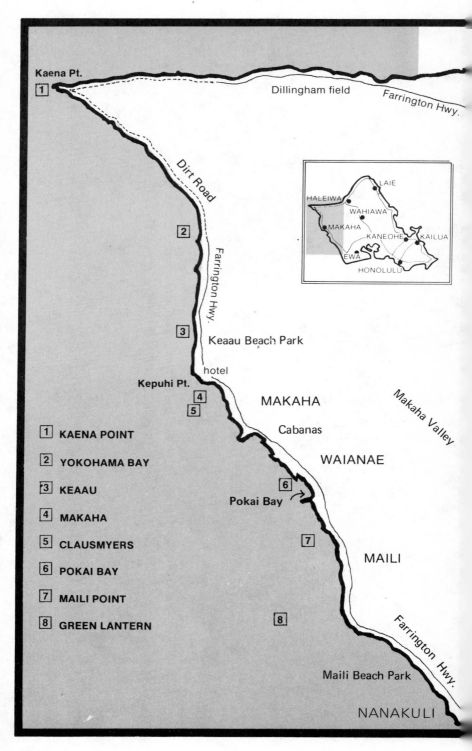

Kaena Pt.

1

Dillingham field

Farrington Hwy.

Dirt Road

Farrington Hwy.

2

3

Keaau Beach Park

hotel

Kepuhi Pt.

4
5

MAKAHA

Cabanas

WAIANAE

6

Pokai Bay

7

MAILI

8

Farrington Hwy.

Maili Beach Park

NANAKULI

Makaha Valley

HALEIWA   LAIE

WAHIAWA

MAKAHA

KANEOHE   KAILUA

EWA

HONOLULU

1 KAENA POINT

2 YOKOHAMA BAY

3 KEAAU

4 MAKAHA

5 CLAUSMYERS

6 POKAI BAY

7 MAILI POINT

8 GREEN LANTERN

A wild, unruly wall thunders overhead as rider prepares to prone out.

KAENA POINT TO NANAKULI

Shoreline: This is Leeward Oahu. The climate is warm and the air is dry. The surfing areas are easily accesible but very crowded.

Wind: Prevailing trades produce warm offshore breezes. Kona winds roar onshore creating bumpy, uneven swells.

Swell: Waves break year 'round. Summer swells produce long, thick lefts while west swells generate powerful rights during winter months.

Notes: This is a very popular coast. On weekends the surfing areas are extremely crowded. . . . Unsuccessful attempts have been made to ride Kaena Point at 40 feet plus.

SURFING AREAS

KAENA POINT

Giant winter waves. 30-60 feet. Largest surf of all islands. As yet unridden!

YOKOHAMA BAY

Fast building peaks. Left over shallow reef. Inside shorebreak. 2-15 feet, south swell. Summer juice.

KEAAU

Long, thick lefts off point. Needs strong swell to work. Rock beach Park nearby. Summer surf.

MAKAHA

Long peeling rights. Bowls during big swells. Takes both north and west swell. Backwash. Best winter spot on leeward side.

Searching for a fast line on a perfect "Pipeline" left.

Locked under tons of whitewater; inside reef "Sunset Beach", Oahu.

CLAUSMEYERS

Shifting lefts across the channel from Makaha. North or west swell. Wintertime.

POKAI BAY

Small beginners surf. Sandy beach. Gentle winter waves.

MAILI POINT

Long rights, 3-20 feet. Requires a large west swell. Breaks during winter months.

GREEN LANTERN

Long lefts during big south swells. Slow rights on west swell. Rocky beach. Easy access. Summer and Winter.

"Big Pipeline" . . . During large surf, the breaking pattern of many areas changes. At the Pipeline 15-20 foot waves break further out on the reef. This produces an unusually mushy take off (see photo) far from the normal top to bottom tube. Not shown is the "outer reef" located ¾ mile offshore. It breaks only on the biggest swells and rarely, if ever, ridden.

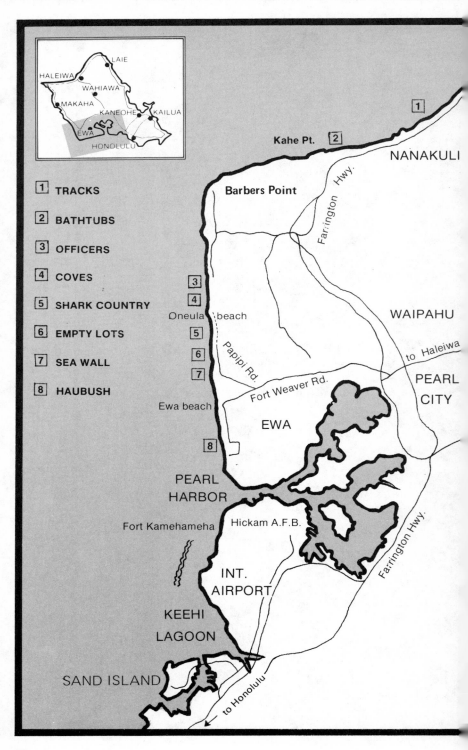

1 TRACKS

2 BATHTUBS

3 OFFICERS

4 COVES

5 SHARK COUNTRY

6 EMPTY LOTS

7 SEA WALL

8 HAUBUSH

A perfect summer swell smokes across a south shore reef.

NANAKULI TO BARBERS POINT

Shoreline: Very little is known about this area. Private property restricts access and entry is by foot or boat.

Wind: Perfect offshore conditions exist most of the year. During kona storms the winds turn onshore and destroys surfing.

Swell: South and west swells generate constant summer and winter surf. Extremely large north swells will occasionally wrap into this area.

Notes: Entry to this coast is by foot from either Kahe or Barbers Point.

SURFING AREAS

TRACKS
Powerful beach peaks. Rights and lefts. West swell. Park and sandy beach. Winter.

BATHTUBS
Short right peaks. In front of power company. Currents. Summer and Winter.

OFFICERS
Small rights and lefts. 2-6 feet. Private Gov't. property. Windy and bumpy. Year 'round waves.

COVES
Short rights and lefts. South or west swell. Surf can be ridden all year.

SHARK COUNTRY
Miscellaneous reef breaks. South or west swell. Noted for its abundance of unfriendly fins. Year 'round waves.

EMPTY LOTS
Short, choppy rights and lefts. Numerous breaks everywhere. Windy. Year 'round.

SEA WALL
Varied reef breaks. Easy rights and lefts. South or west swell. Surfable year 'round.

HAUBUSH
Gentle lefts but usually choppy. Needs a north wind. Surf breaks all year.

BARBERS POINT TO PEARL HARBOR

Shoreline: Parks and beaches allow access to all surfing areas along Ewa Beach. . . . Irregular reef formations produce poor and unreliable wave shape.

Wind: Seas are blownout most of the year. Only during a rare north wind will offshore conditions prevail.

Swell: South and west swells generate constant but poorly shaped surf.

Notes: Sewage and deep water attract sharks—keep eyes peeled.

PEARL HARBOR TO SAND ISLAND

Shoreline: Due to government property and airport facilities access to the flawless tubes is very difficult. The outer reefs can be reached by boat or long paddle.

Wind: Ideal offshores can be relied upon most of the year. Kona storms create destructive onshore breezes.

Swell: Summer and winter swells produce uncrowded perfection along this rarely surfed coastline.

Notes: A sewage outlet attracts sharks — keep eyes peeled for unfriendly fins.

Banking below a large "Pupukea" section — north shore, Oahu.

New hotel under construction near Kahuku town on the island of Oahu.

CORAL

The coral reefs are made up of millions of tiny organisms, each of which forms a hard, skeletal, limestone shell around itself. A reef might be vaguely compared with some kind of natural apartment complex, with the center or base of the reef composed of empty shells from previous generations of coral, and the outside composed of the living, current generation.

The coral itself, inside the limestone shell, has a soft hollow body and tenacles surrounding a central mouth. It feeds on small and microscopic organisms, and except for the skeletal structure, is closely related to the sea anemone.

The limestone shell is what makes the coral so dangerous for surfers and swimmers. Especially in places where the coral has been broken off, leaving jagged chunks sharp enough to cause deep lacerations. The cut resulting from coral is not in itself as dangerous, as the microscopic bacteria which may get under the skin and cause serious infection — known as coral poisoning.

To avoid this, never walk over reefs — rather, paddle the board upside down or find a channel around the reef. If you are swimming, use a shallow breast stroke until you are past the reef.

If you get cut, clean the wound carefully with a good antiseptic. If it doesn't seem to be healing within a week, or if infection sets in, **see a doctor.**

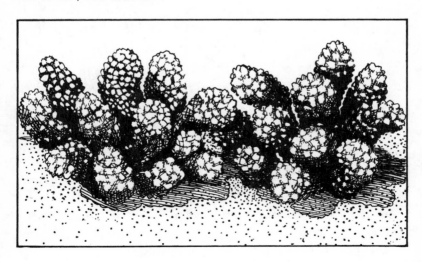

SEA URCHINS

In Hawaii, sea urchins are called **"vana"**. They resemble fat purple pincushions with long needles sticking outwards. **These needles** are actually hollow spines and serve as a protective device to ward off predators. The length of these brittle spines ranges from one to six inches, depending on the size of the sea urchin.

If you should step on one, try to pull the spines out of your skin without breaking them off. Any portion that breaks off and remains under your skin can cause infection.

If the spines do break off, soaking in hot water and epsom salts will relieve the pain and make it easier to remove the spines. If the pain persists or if infection sets in, see a doctor.

 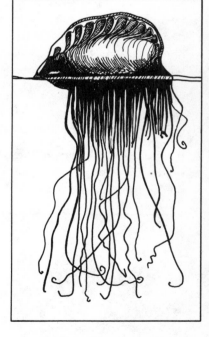

PORTUGUESE MAN-O'-WAR

This large, colorful jellyfish drifts on the surface of the sea by means of a sail-like float, filled with gas. The sail is blue in color, with a pink or crimson crest. Under the float hang long, blue, poisonous tentacles, which can reach a length of 60 to 100 feet in the larger specimens.

It is the tenacles that make this jellyfish so feared. Just one thimbleful of the poison could kill 1000 mice. However, when a human being is stung, very little poison is injected — but the pain is still excruciating and a severe sting can cause collapse.

It is **not common** to see these creatures in the surf — they are usually swept shorewards during a period of high winds.

If you are stung by a MAN-O'-WAR, and if nothing else is available, rub the wound with wet sand and cleanse it thoroughly. If possible, bathe the wound in alcohol or vinegar. The pain usually lasts about 30 to 40 minutes. To ease the burning sensation, you can try a cold compress or just plain ice. You can also use ammonia or calamine lotion — these should be applied with a clean rag or cotton swab.

In cases where a severe sting causes collapse, medical attention should be sought immediately, and treatment for shock should be given to the victim.

SHARKS

The shark has one of the most fearsome reputations of all sea creatures. Its appearance in the water can panic the experienced swimmer or surfer. With its streamlined body, half-moon shaped mouth, and razor sharp teeth, it is easy to see why it is so feared.

The most common species of shark found in Hawaiian waters are the Sandbar, Grey, and Hammerhead. They live outside the reef and seldom venture inside because of the turbulent wave action.

The shark is a carniverous animal, to whom the sight of a surfer's dangling legs might prove an irrestible lure. However, few species attack humans and the few incidents of attack are regarded as extraordinary events.

In most meetings between shark and man, the shark will cruise on past, perhaps circling once out of curiosity. REMEMBER, the shark is unpredictable and never seems to need a reason to attack. Never count on a shark cruising on past, watch him closely and calmly get back to shore. Don't panic, a thrashing human makes an attractive target for a hungry shark.

The shark has an extraordinary sense of smell. The scent of blood draws him quickly. He can also pick up low frequency sound and vibrations in the water. This is the reason he appears so quickly when another fish is in trouble. The thrashing movements send out vibrations which the shark translates to "easy prey".

Before a shark attacks, it cautiously circles its victim, gradually swimming in smaller and smaller circles until it eventually bumps the victim with its snout. If it seems like easy prey, the next time he will attack.

If you are ever the possible victim of an attack, the important thing is **NOT TO PANIC**. If the shark persists, an effective defense is direct blows on his sensitive nose. After you have driven him off, warn others in the vicinity and swim calmly to shore. Shouting will not drive the shark away.

BASIC RULES

1. Don't swim alone.

2. Don't swim at night or in murky waters.

3. Don't stay in the water with a bleeding wound.

4. Don't panic or thrash around. Get to the beach.

5. If a shark moves in on you, hit it on the nose.

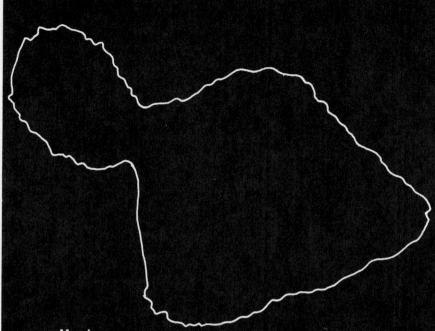

Maui . . .
the valley isle,
island of many faces;
boasting dusty old Lahaina,
and Hana,
lushly tucked away;
where Olinda and Kula warm the evening
with fireplace
and rambling pasture lands stretch like patchwork
among the eucalyptus trees;

. . . where every surfer "gets it on"
at Honalua Bay, Malo Wharf,
or Maalea Harbor's "freight train right";
where no surfer can say he's truly been
'til he can say that he's "dropped in"
Haleakala Crater;

. . . where every road invites you,
every day delights you;
where the love with which you have to live
depends upon how much you have to give.

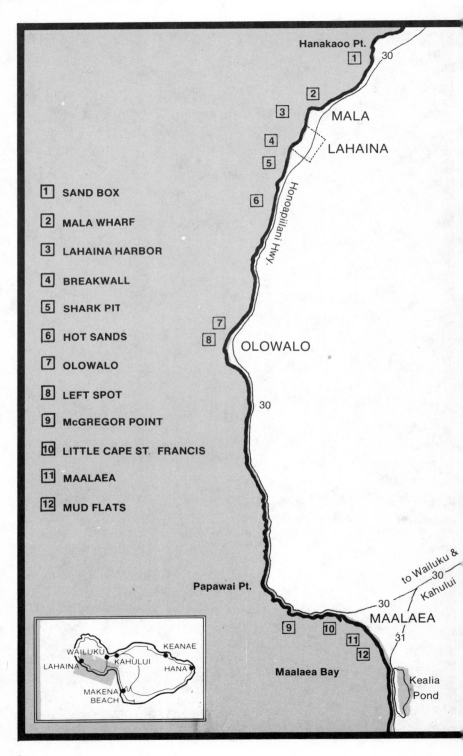

Hanakaoo Pt.

30

1

2

3

MALA

LAHAINA

4

5

6

Honoapiilani Hwy.

1 SAND BOX

2 MALA WHARF

3 LAHAINA HARBOR

4 BREAKWALL

5 SHARK PIT

6 HOT SANDS

7 OLOWALO

8 LEFT SPOT

9 McGREGOR POINT

10 LITTLE CAPE ST. FRANCIS

11 MAALAEA

12 MUD FLATS

7

8

OLOWALO

30

to Wailuku &

30

Kahului

30

MAALAEA

31

Papawai Pt.

9

10

11

12

Maalaea Bay

Kealia Pond

WAILUKU

KAHULUI

KEANAE

LAHAINA

HANA

MAKENA
BEACH

50

A sweeping bottom turn helps avoid a thick section of whitewater.

Shoreline: Rocky points and white sand beaches extend along Maui's popular south shore. Parks and coastal roads provide access to the surfing areas.

Wind: Warm tradewinds create ideal offshore conditions. The rare kona winds generate onshore breezes.

Swell: Surfing is best during Summer. South swells wrap into the bays producing long, cylindrical tubes. . . . Strong west swells sometimes generate small winter surf.

Notes: Unstable trades can be expected along Maalaea Bay. . . . Rock and coral cover the reefs — use caution while surfing at low tide.

SURFING AREAS

SAND BOX
Clean rights. Need big winter swell to work. Best 2-4 feet. Surfable when all is closed out.

MALA WARF
Long, thin lefts. South swell, 2-12 feet. Best during Summer.

LAHAINA HARBOR
Soft right shoulder. Long thin left. Harbor entrance. 1-7 feet, summer swell.

BREAKWALL
Hollow lefts in front of seawall. Hightide best. 2-8 feet, south swell.

SHARK PIT.

Shark breeding grounds. Lefts, some rights. Shallow reef. South swell. Summer spot.

HOT SANDS

Small peaks. Right slide. Best on 2-6 foot south swell. Summer.

OLOWALO

Soft peaks, right and left. Shallow reef at low tide. Best on south swell but big north will work too. Summer and Winter.

LEFT SPOT

Fast, hollow lefts. Medium south swell, 2-8 feet. Summer surf spot.

McGREGOR POINT

Long point rights. Needs 5-10 foot south swell. Warm summer juice.

LITTLE CAPE ST. FRANCIS

Long right walls off point. Endless tubes. Needs 5-10 foot south swell. Summer surf.

MAALAEA

"Freight train rights." Infinite walls. 3-12 foot south swell. Best area on south shore.

MUD FLATS

Radical rights. 2-8 feet, south swell. Dangerous reef at low tide. Summer spot.

Riding high on a soft summer curl — "Left Spot", Maui.

South swell juice pumps across a Maui reef.

"The Bay" . . . Waimea Bay is a peak break followed by a thunderous right shoulder. The ride ends when the wave enters a deep water canyon (see diagram page 32). The initial take-off is critical. As the onrushing swell hits the reef, it sucks out producing almost a vertical drop from crest to trough. The abrupt drop, fierce offshore wind and a bumpy surface make riding "The Bay" hazardous (to say the least). Each year, only a handful of men challenge its strength.

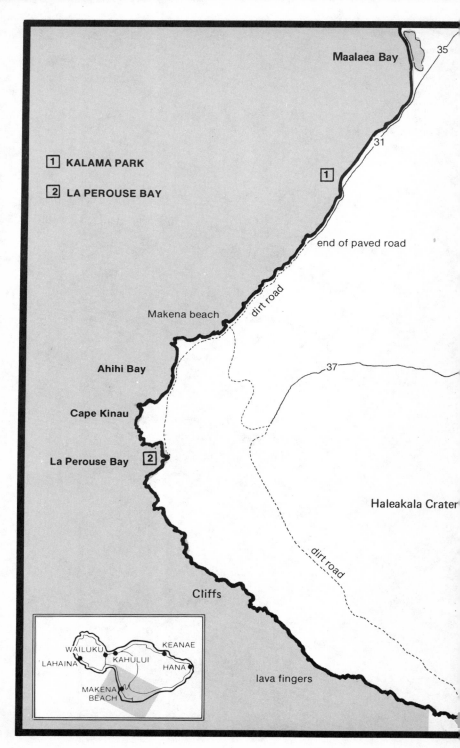

Maalaea Bay

35

31

1 KALAMA PARK

2 LA PEROUSE BAY

1

end of paved road

dirt road

Makena beach

Ahihi Bay

37

Cape Kinau

La Perouse Bay 2

Haleakala Crater

dirt road

Cliffs

lava fingers

WAILUKU — KEANAE
LAHAINA — KAHULUI — HANA
MAKENA
BEACH

54

Shoreline: Parks and sandy beaches provide easy access to the reefs between Maalaea and Makena Beach. Steep cliffs extend from Makena to La Perouse Bay where the coastal road abruptly ends.

Wind: Warm trades produce offshore surfing conditions. Variable gusts are common.

Swell: South swells produce warm tubes during the hot summer days. Powerful west swells sometimes generate unexpected winter waves.

Notes: Cliffs and razor sharp lava make surfing at La Perouse Bay a bit risky. . . . When winter swells create surf along this shore, the riding direction will change (rights become lefts, etc.).

SURFING AREAS

KALAMA PARK
Right and lefts over coral reef. 3-8 feet, south swell. Summer break.

LA PEROUSE BAY
"A Sunset left." Steep and hairy. Needs 10-15 foot south swell. Lava fingers. Experts only. Summer.

High on the lip, exploring for pockets of untapped power.

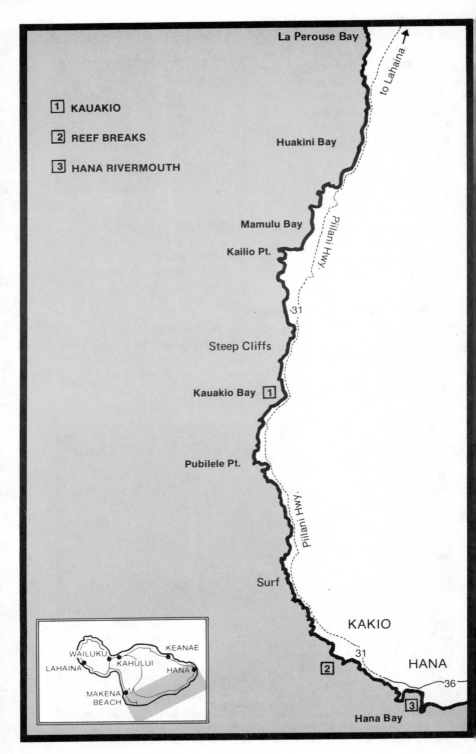

1 KAUAKIO

2 REEF BREAKS

3 HANA RIVERMOUTH

La Perouse Bay

to Lahaina

Huakini Bay

Mamulu Bay

Kailio Pt.

Piilani Hwy.

31

Steep Cliffs

Kauakio Bay 1

Pubilele Pt.

Piilani Hwy.

Surf

KAKIO

31

HANA

2

36

3

Hana Bay

KEANAE
WAILUKU
KAHULUI
LAHAINA
HANA
MAKENA
BEACH

A summer tube smokes along the south shore of Maui.

LA PEROUSE BAY TO KAKIO

Shoreline: Cliffs and rocky shores extend the length of this coast. Access to the sea is limited to a few small seaside villages.

Wind: Gusty tradewinds turn the ocean surface to churning white caps. Smooth seas can sometimes be found in the mornings or evenings.

Swell: High-powered south swells send surf crashing onto the rocky shores. Winter swells fail to reach this side of Maui.

Notes: Ragged lava fingers make surfing extremely risky.

HANA

Shoreline: The jagged cliffs turn to rolling slopes as the narrow dirt road approaches Hana. Access to the uncrowded reefs is through numerous parks and sandy beaches.

Wind: The warm trades create constant offshore riding conditions. The occasional kona winds will quickly destroy the ocean surface .

Swell: South swells produce fast, clean, summer tubes. Wind swells generate small, choppy surf during winter months.

Notes: The shape of the waves found in Hana is similar to those of Mexico.

SURFING AREAS

KAUAKIO
Point lefts, 2-6 feet. South swell. Lava and steep cliffs. Rarely surfed. Summer.

REEF BREAKS
Tubular peaks, right and left. Shallow reef. 1-8 feet. Summer surf spot.

HANA BAY RIVERMOUTH
Soft, gentle lefts. 2-6 feet. Breaks Summer and Winter.

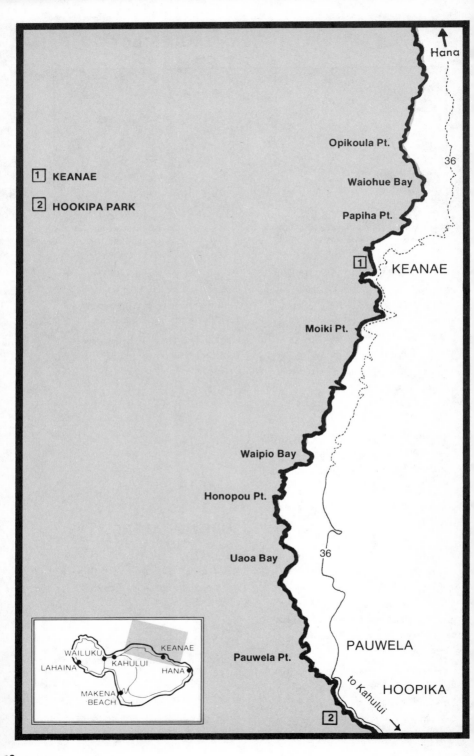

1 KEANAE

2 HOOKIPA PARK

Hana

Opikoula Pt.

Waiohue Bay

Papiha Pt.

36

1 KEANAE

Moiki Pt.

Waipio Bay

Honopou Pt.

Uaoa Bay

36

PAUWELA

Pauwela Pt.

to Kahului

HOOPIKA

WAILUKU   KEANAE
LAHAINA KAHULUI
                HANA
MAKENA
BEACH

2

A low center of gravity helps when takeoffs are steep and the wind roars up the face.

Jamming high off a bursting lip, Maui.

Shoreline: Steep, rocky coastline extends from Hana to Hookipa Park. The twisting highway runs far inland and side trips must be taken to reach the sea.

Wind: The northeast trades strike head-on producing bumpy and uneven seas. Kona winds blow offshore and fantastic surfing conditions usually result.

Swell: Northern storms produce powerful winter juice. East wind swells cause bumpy summer surf.

Notes: A combination of north swell and kona wind will produce fabulous surf. Caution, strong rips exist during these times.

SURFING AREAS

KEANAE
Fast and bumpy rights. 4-8 feet. North or East swell. Winter spot.

HOOKIPA PARK
Strong left walls. Needs giant north swell. Dangerous currents. Long paddle. Summer and Winter.

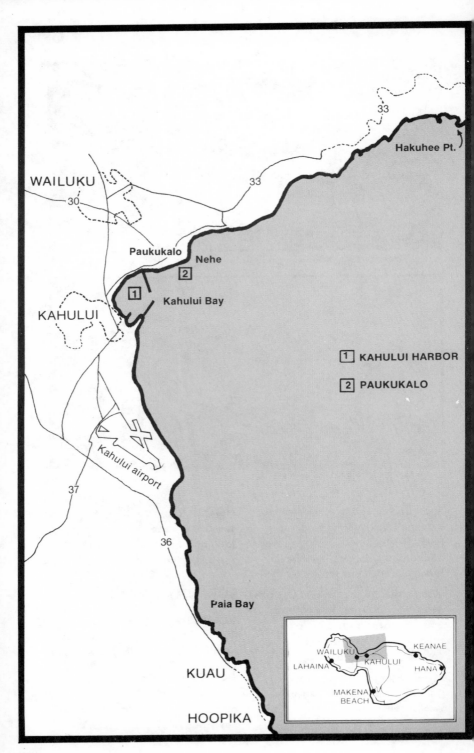

WAILUKU

30

Paukukalo

Nehe

2

1

Kahului Bay

KAHULUI

33

Hakuhee Pt.

33

1 KAHULUI HARBOR

2 PAUKUKALO

Kahului airport

37

36

Paia Bay

KUAU

HOOPIKA

WAILUKU   KAHULUI   KEANAE
LAHAINA   HANA
          MAKENA
          BEACH

Shoreline: The winding road from Hana meets the sea near Hookipa Park. From here to Kahalui the coast is level and the surfing areas easily reached. . . . North of Wailuku town, the road again climbs into the hills and begins a long twisting journey to Kaanapali.

Wind: Onshore trades produce junky surface conditions most of the year. When the winds are from the south (kona) surfing will be fantastic.

Swell: North and west swells generate powerful surf along this coast. . . . During summer months, east wind swells produce small but ridable waves.

Notes: Razor sharp reefs lurk below the surface—avoid contact at all costs. . . . Dangerous currents are created during large winter surf.

SURFING AREAS

KAHULUI HARBOR
Thin, quick lefts. 2-6 feet, north swell. Inside harbor. Needs kona winds. Wintertime.

PUAKUKALO
Powerful lefts off point. 2-15 feet. North swell. Kona wind. Winter surf.

Goofyfooter carves tracks as he accelerates below the feathering crest.

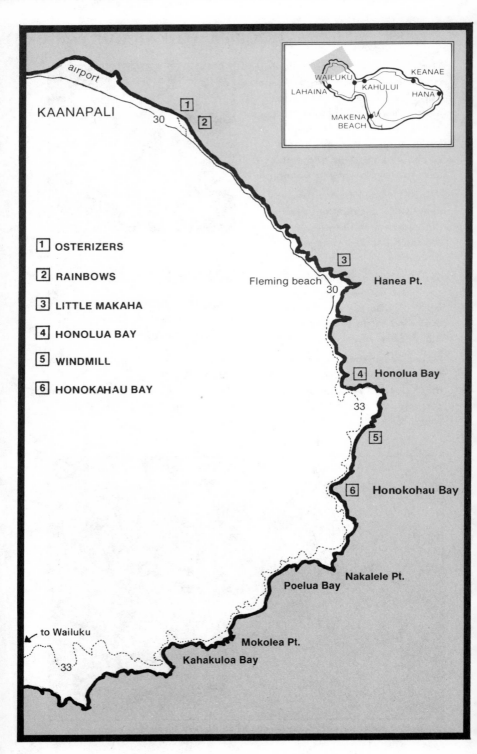

KAANAPALI

airport

30

1 **OSTERIZERS**

2 **RAINBOWS**

3 **LITTLE MAKAHA**

4 **HONOLUA BAY**

5 **WINDMILL**

6 **HONOKAHAU BAY**

Fleming beach

30

Hanea Pt.

4 Honolua Bay

33

5

6 Honokohau Bay

Nakalele Pt.

Poelua Bay

to Wailuku

33

Mokolea Pt.

Kahakuloa Bay

WAILUKU
LAHAINA
KAHULUI
KEANAE
HANA
MAKENA
BEACH

Shoreline: Abrupt cliffs and rocky shores extend along this northern coast. Small dirt roads often lead toward the sea but access to the surf is extremely difficult. . . .
The surf spots between Honolua Bay and Lahaina are easier to reach. Parks, beaches and coast roads provide easy access.

Wind: Between Wailuku and Honokohau Bay the trades blow onshore. Only during kona winds will these waters be surfable. . . .
A short distance past Honokohau, the trades roar out to sea leaving the points and bays that follow with constant offshore smoothness.

Swell: High-powered north and west swells blast this coast during winter months. The summer months are calm without a ripple.

Notes: Contact with the reefs is extremely dangerous. . . . Because of its geographical position, Maui's surf is 2 to 3 feet smaller than on the other islands.

SURFING AREAS

OSTERIZERS
Churning right tubes. 2-8 feet, north or west swell. Off main highway. Uncrowded. Winter spot.

RAINBOWS
Long, radical tubes. North or west swell. Winter surf spot.

LITTLE MAKAHA
Clean, fast rights, 3-10 foot north or west swell. Winter perfection.

HONOLUA BAY
Smoking right tube. Long and hollow. Grinding inside bowl. A perfect wave. Closes at 15 feet. Best spot on North Shore.

WINDMILL
A flawless peak. Left or right. North or West swell. Usually uncrowded. Winter surf.

HONOKOHAU
A muscular right. 2-12 feet, winter swell. Wind, tide, swell very critical. Northern juice.

Fully extended into a thick, winter curl.

TIDES

The natural movement of the tides has a direct effect upon surfing in the Hawaiian Islands. The difference between high and low tide will many times determine where, when, and if you surf at all.

Depending on the size of the swell, many surfing areas will be ridable at low tide but not at high. For example, a three foot wave will break over many reefs when the tide is out, but at high tide the greater amount of water between reef and wave crest will prevent this same wave from breaking.

Tides also affect the **shape** of waves. At lower tides, the waves tend to line-up, breaking top-to-bottom with very little riding area (see diagram). At high tide, the larger volume of water produces a thicker wave with a greater surfing area (see diagram).

It is important to remember that at low tide many reefs are partially exposed. Coral, vana, and sharp rocks are found close to the ocean's surface. When these conditions exist — wait for high tide.

This is general knowledge which will help you to better understand and enjoy Hawaiian waves. Only by actually experiencing the natural elements will you learn the particulars of each spot.

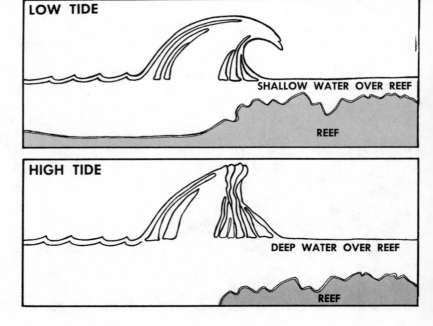

LOW TIDE

SHALLOW WATER OVER REEF

REEF

HIGH TIDE

DEEP WATER OVER REEF

REEF

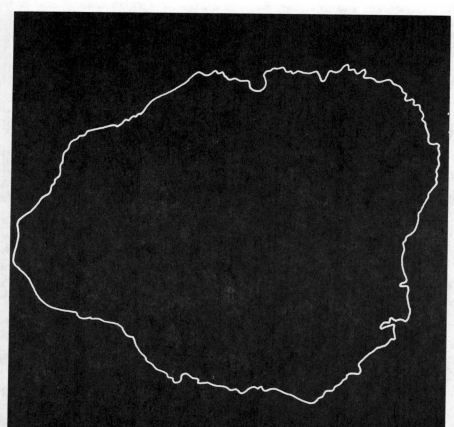

Kauai . . .

       appropriately named the garden isle,
       where fruit and flowers decorate the way to every set;
       where seven major rivers
       keep the island wet;

       If Hanalei and Pakala
       show no swell,
       visit Waimea Canyon for a stretch of the imagination,
       or Kalalau Valley for a stretch of the hiking legs
       through a tropical paradise.

       . . . where traces of a pre-Hawaiian civilization
       lay claim to the oldest history of the islands . . .

       . . . where slow is the scene
       and peace of mind — is every day routine.

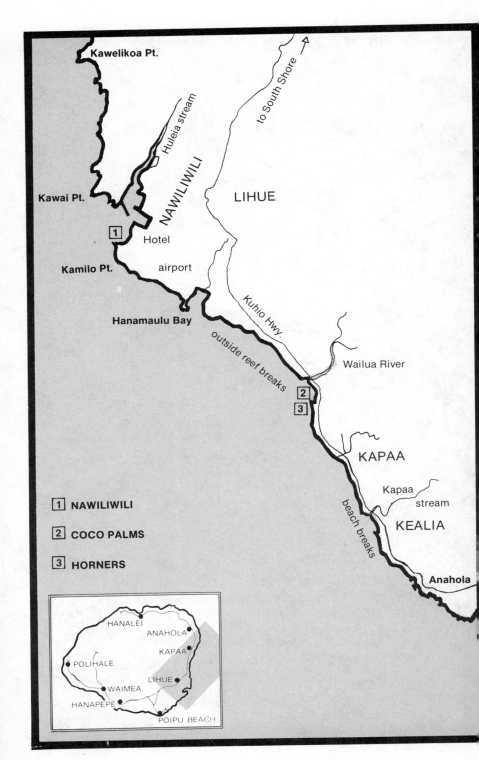

Kawelikoa Pt.

Huleia stream

NAWILIWILI

Kawai Pt.

to South Shore

LIHUE

1

Hotel

Kamilo Pt.

airport

Hanamaulu Bay

Kuhio Hwy.

outside reef breaks

Wailua River

2
3

KAPAA

Kapaa
stream

1 NAWILIWILI

2 COCO PALMS

3 HORNERS

beach breaks

KEALIA

Anahola

HANALEI
ANAHOLA
KAPAA
POLIHALE
LIHUE
WAIMEA
HANAPEPE
POIPU BEACH

Quick, explosive tubes require properly designed equipment.

Shoreline: Large sections of this coast are privately owned and access to many surfable points is difficult. . . . Scattered along this coast are numerous surfing and bodysurfing breaks.

Wind: This is windward Kauai. The northeast trades blow onshore producing bumpy surf most of the year. The offshore kona winds will generate uncrowded perfection.

Swell: Ridable surf can always be found. North and east swells produce choppy but constant waves.

Notes: Strong ocean swells produce fantastic bodysurfing along many sandy beaches.

SURFING AREAS

NAWILIWILI BAY
Small point surf inside bay. Gentle beginners waves. Summertime.

COCO PALMS
Fast, tubular peaks. Usually bumpy. Excellent bodysurfing. Sandy bottom. Breaks Summer and Winter.

HORNERS
Thick left shoulders. Best during kona winds. Usually choppy. Works year 'round.

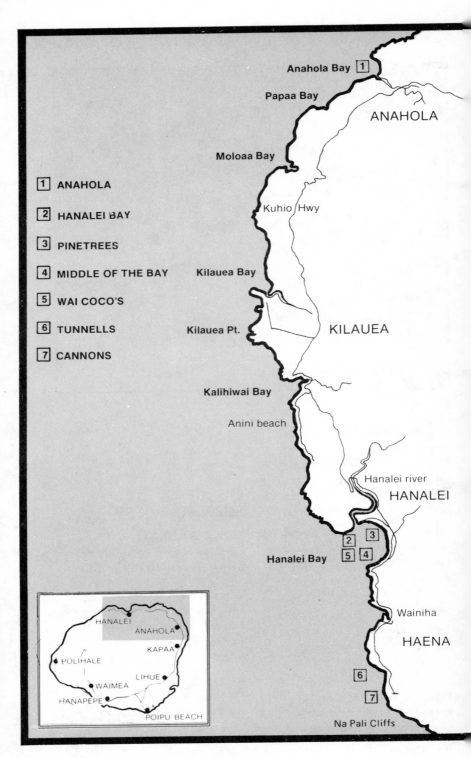

1 ANAHOLA

2 HANALEI BAY

3 PINETREES

4 MIDDLE OF THE BAY

5 WAI COCO'S

6 TUNNELLS

7 CANNONS

Anahola Bay 1

Papaa Bay

ANAHOLA

Moloaa Bay

Kuhio Hwy

Kilauea Bay

Kilauea Pt.

KILAUEA

Kalihiwai Bay

Anini beach

Hanalei river

HANALEI

2 3

5 4

Hanalei Bay

Wainiha

HAENA

6

7

Na Pali Cliffs

HANALEI
ANAHOLA
KAPAA
POLIHALE
LIHUE
WAIMEA
HANAPEPE
POIPU BEACH

Siipping left as tube begins to throw — north shore, Oahu.

Shoreline: Most of the land between Anahola and Hanalei Bay is privately owned. Access to this rocky, windswept shoreline is difficult and usually not worth the effort. . . . Parks and white sand beaches dot the coast from Hanalei to Haena. Points and bays offer various conditions— from the pumping rights of 'Hanalei Bay'' to the radical lefts of "Cannons."

Wind: Between Anahola and Kilauea the trades roar onshore. Blownout conditions prevail. . . . A short distance past Kilauea, the trades blow out to sea. The surfing areas that follow experience almost constant off-shore winds.

Swell: This is the north shore. North and west swells generate steep and powerful winter tubes. Summer swells do not reach this coast.

Notes: Kauai is tempermental. Winds and swells are un-predictable. But when nature's forces are in harmony, fantastic surf will result.

SURFING AREAS

ANAHOLA
Rights off a small point. Shallow reef. Needs kona wind. Breaks year 'round.

HANALEI BAY

Long right walls. 2-20 feet, winter swell. Three take-off spots. Wicked inside bowl. Winter juice.

PINETREES

Smoking left tubes. Needs perfect conditions to work. Breaks only in winter months.

MIDDLE OF THE BAY

Strong lefts. 3-12 feet, winter swell. Currents inside. Usually choppy. Winter.

WAI COCO'S

Bruising lefts off point. Requires ideal wind and swell. Across from Hanalei Bay. Winter perfection.

TUNNELS

Screaming rights. 2-10 foot cylinders. Windy. Sharp reef. North or west swell.

CANNONS

Explosive lefts over shallow reef. 1/4 mile out. Strong currents inside. Takes north or west swell. Winter juice.

Searching for the fast line as tunnel takes shape.

Chambers of juice can be found near the bursting lip.

"Aluetian Juice"... Fierce storms in the north and west Pacific produce powerful and constant winter surf. With the big waves come strong tradewinds (see photo) making takeoffs extremely difficult. By the second or third day the winds usually die, the sea smooths and calm conditions prevail. These storms produce the best surf along coastlines facing north or west.

71

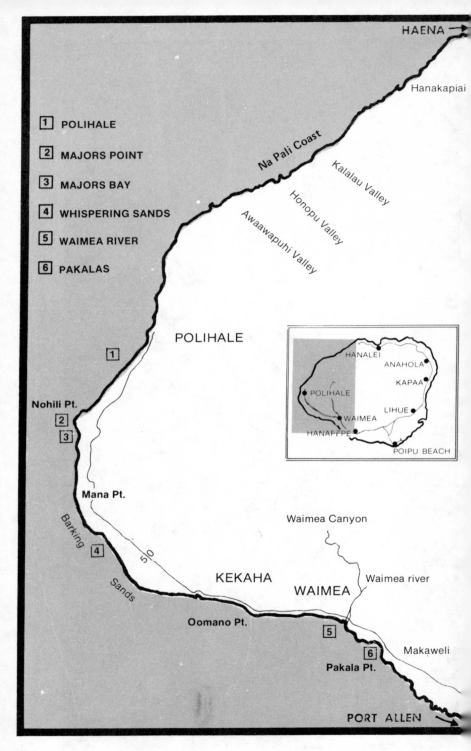

1 POLIHALE
2 MAJORS POINT
3 MAJORS BAY
4 WHISPERING SANDS
5 WAIMEA RIVER
6 PAKALAS

HAENA

Hanakapiai

Na Pali Coast

Kalalau Valley

Honopu Valley

Awaawapuhi Valley

POLIHALE

1

Nohili Pt.
2
3

Mana Pt.

Barking

Sands

4

50

KEKAHA

WAIMEA

Waimea Canyon

Waimea river

Oomano Pt.

5

Pakala Pt.
6

Makaweli

PORT ALLEN

HANALEI
ANAHOLA
KAPAA
POLIHALE
LIHUE
WAIMEA
HANAPEPE
POIPU BEACH

Squeezed tight as a heavy lip pours forth.

HAENA TO POLIHALE

Shoreline: This is Kauai's famous Na-Pali coast. Sheer cliffs and rock beaches make surfing impossible.

POLIHALE TO KEKAHA

Shoreline: Government land extends along this coast and entry to the surfable beaches is restricted. . . . Near the small town of Kekaha, various reef breaks produce small, fast waves.

Wind: Sidewinds produce favorabe surface conditions most of the year. Kona storms bring choppy, unmanagable seas.

Swell: North and west swells generate strong surf during winter months. South swells fail to reach this shoreline.

Notes: Dangerous rip-currents are created as swells bounce off the cliffs — exercise extreme caution before entering the water at Polihale.

SURFING AREAS

POLIHALE

Thick, explosive peaks. Lefts and rights. Beach break. Strong currents inside. Experts only. Winter months.

MAJORS POINT

Long right lines off point. On government property. Takes west swell. Wintertime.

MAJORS BAY

Soft peaks — right and left. Government property. Difficult to find. West swell. Winter.

WHISPERING SANDS

Flawless tubes. Usually uncrowded. Difficult to find. West swell. Winter months.

KEKAHA TO PORT ALLEN

Shoreline: Although highway 50 runs parallel with the sea, many surfing reefs cannot be reached. Trespassing laws are strictly enforced along miles of private beachfront. To reach the perfection lefts of "Infinities", a hefty 2 mile hike is required.

Wind: The tradewinds are unpredictable. In minutes they can change from offshore breezes to onshore gusts.

Swell: Both south and west swells produce ridable year 'round surf.

Notes: Waste from the sugar mills attract numerous sharks to these waters.

SURFING AREAS

WAIMEA RIVERMOUTH

Rights and lefts. Reef breaks. 2-8 feet, south or west swell.
Variable winds. Sharks and dirty water. Summer and Winter.

PAKALAS/INFINITIES

Long, unspoiled lefts. Works on south or west swell. Shifty winds. Sharks. Other breaks in area.
Two mile hike required. Summer and Winter.

Rotating high into feathering Kauai curl.

Driving cutback as wave backs off in deep water.

Perfection at "Sunset Beach" . . . Riding conditions are ideal; a 12-15 foot swell, offshore wind and solitude. The peak is working. A steep, elevator take-off followed by a smoking right shoulder with a possible inside section (not shown). **Note:** The left slide looks makeable but isn't! The boil (extreme right) indicates a shallow reef and the lefts usually end at that point.

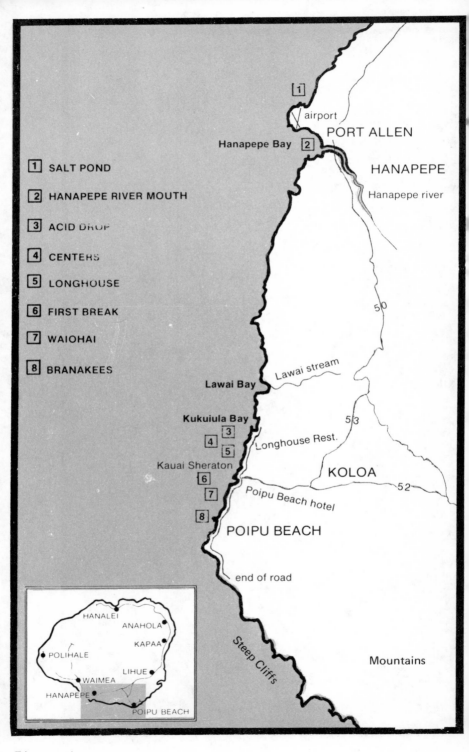

1 SALT POND

2 HANAPEPE RIVER MOUTH

3 ACID DROP

4 CENTERS

5 LONGHOUSE

6 FIRST BREAK

7 WAIOHAI

8 BRANAKEES

1 airport
PORT ALLEN
Hanapepe Bay 2
HANAPEPE
Hanapepe river

50

Lawai stream
Lawai Bay

Kukuiula Bay
3
4
5
Longhouse Rest.
53
Kauai Sheraton
6
KOLOA
7
Poipu Beach hotel
52
8
POIPU BEACH

end of road

Steep Cliffs

Mountains

HANALEI
ANAHOLA
KAPAA
POLIHALE
LIHUE
WAIMEA
HANAPEPE
POIPU BEACH

Stroking for the edge as rider outside bears down — "Pipeline Rights", Oahu.

Shoreline: Past Port Allen, highway 50 turns east heading inland. Little is known of the coast and surfing areas between Port Allen and Poipu. . . . Poipu Beach is a south shore resort area. During Summer, the surf spots along this shore produce hollow, warm tubes. Parks and sandy beaches allow easy access. . . . The land between Poipu and Nawiliwili is privately owned and entry is restricted.

Wind: Offshore tradewinds blow with unpredictable strength. In seconds, a five knot breeze can gust to twenty. Early mornings and late evenings produce the best wave conditions.

Swell: South swells produce warm summer juice. For some reason the surf is usually 2 to 3 feet bigger here than on the other islands.

Notes: Beware of swift currents that flow between "Longhouse" and "Acid Drop". . . . Coral and sharp rocks cover the reefs — avoid stepping into unknown depths.

SURFING AREAS

SALT POND
Right and left reef breaks. 2-10 foot south swell. Constant offshore winds. Beach Park. Clean summer tubes.

HANAPEPE RIVERMOUTH
Countless small reef breaks. Rocky shoreline. Strong currents. Sharks and dirty water. Not recommended for surfing.

ACID DROP
Steep, hollow peak. Right or left. Needs a 3-10 foot south swell. Strong inside currents. Lava beach. Summertime.

CENTERS
Smooth right peak working into an inside tube. Shallow coral reef. Strong currents inside. Takes south swell. Summertime.

LONGHOUSE
Long, hollow left — short, mushy right. Breaks 2-8 feet, south swell. Strong currents. Summer juice.

FIRST BREAK
Steep, right peak. Needs 5-10 foot south swell. Deep reef. $\frac{1}{2}$ mile out. Summer power.

WAIOHAI
Thick left off point. Hollow inside tube. Shallow coral reef. Best at high tide. Summer surf. Crowded.

BRANEKEES
Bodysurfing beach. Crushing shorebreak. Sandy bottom. Center of summer activity.

A glass smooth tube pours over as surfer makes for the outside.

A big left readies to dump as rider looks for a safe path.

A good way to see and enjoy Hawaii is by camping out. During Summer the weather is ideal, warm with little rain. You'll be able to experience first hand the natural beauty the islands have to offer. The winter months are trying. Heavy rains and pesky mosquitoes make camping a task.

You may camp at any public beach park **where camping is permitted**. The following are some basic facts you'll need to know:

1. A camping permit is required. There is no charge for this permit and you may pick one up at any local Parks and Recreation office.

2. All public campgrounds are equipped with restrooms, showers, drinking water, picnic tables, fire pits and shelters.

3. Trailers and campers are permitted at all parks where camping is allowed, but no electrical or sewer connections are provided for these vehicles.

If you need more information, stop by the local Department of Parks and Recreation and pick up a copy of their camping guide. It lists each public park and its facilities and includes a map with the park's exact location.

"The Pipe" . . . Pictured above is the Pipeline located along the north coast of Oahu. Here, massive pacific swells explode over a shallow (5-8 feet) coral reef. Timing is critical. After an almost vertical take-off, the rider must peak and hold a tight left line on the lip.

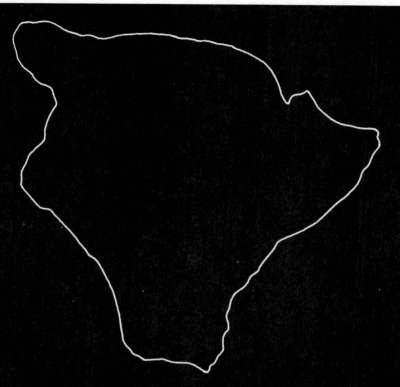

Hawaii . . .
      the big island,
      surfer's virgin hinterland,
      where Mauna Kea/Mauna Loa
      top it with a winterland;
      where . . . when the surf is down
      and the snow is up . . .
      try ski;

      . . . where Hilo grows quietly wet,
      Kailua-Kona harbors the fishing set;
      where Kamuela lies greenly nestled
      in a New England setting . . .
      unchanging . . .

      . . . where miles of highway
      and miles of beach
      so much to see
      is all within reach.

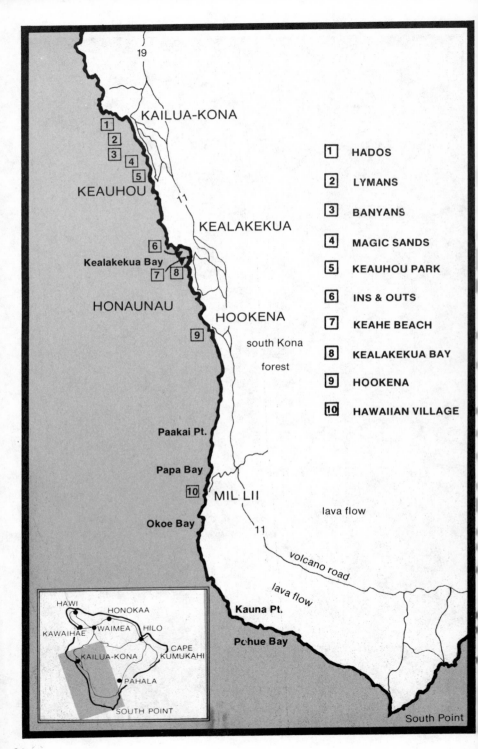

KAILUA-KONA

1	HADOS
2	LYMANS
3	BANYANS
4	MAGIC SANDS
5	KEAUHOU PARK
6	INS & OUTS
7	KEAHE BEACH
8	KEALAKEKUA BAY
9	HOOKENA
10	HAWAIIAN VILLAGE

KEAUHOU

KEALAKEKUA

Kealakekua Bay

HONAUNAU

HOOKENA

south Kona

forest

Paakai Pt.

Papa Bay

MIL LII

Okoe Bay

lava flow

volcano road

lava flow

Kauna Pt.

Pohue Bay

South Point

HAWI
HONOKAA
KAWAIHAE
WAIMEA
HILO
KAILUA-KONA
CAPE
KUMUKAHI
PAHALA
SOUTH POINT

82

Boards built for speed are needed for the long walls of Winter — "Laniakea", Oahu.

Shoreline: Beach parks and coastal roads allow easy access to most of Kona's gold coast. . . . South of town, steep cliffs and fields of raw lava restrict access to the sea. . . . Surfable waves can be found where narrow sideroads lead to the sea.

Wind: Conditions are ideal. Glassy and smooth shape prevails nearly year 'round. . . . During kona storms, the water's surface becomes choppy and \unridable.

Swell: The Kona Coast is blessed with year 'round surf. South swells generate clean summer tubes and potent west swells produce strong winter walls.

Notes: Sharp coral and lava lurk beneath the surface — use extreme caution before stepping down. . . . Countless surf spots exist between Miloii and South Point. Access is by foot or boat.

SURFING AREAS

HADOS
3-10 foot rights. Lava beach. First area south of Kailua-Kona. Summer and Winter.

LYMANS
Clean lefts off a rocky point. 3-10 feet, south swell. Lava. Deep channel. Breaks year 'round.

BANYANS
Peaks, right and left. Shallow reef, easy to be picked off. Best spot on Kona side. Year 'round.

MAGIC SANDS BEACH
Top to bottom bodysurfing. Shorebreak. White sand beach (sometimes). Summer spot.

KEAUHOU PARK
Rights and lefts over shallow reef. 2-8 feet. Rarely works. Summer.

INS & OUTS
Shorebreak of Kealakekua Bay.
Ride in, ride out. High tide.
Summer or Winter.

KEAHE BEACH
Long, firm left off south point of
Kealakekua Bay. 3-10 feet,
south swell.

KEALAKEKUA BAY
Long, left lines off point. Needs 5
feet to work. Summer swells.

HOOKENA
Left. 2-8 feet, south swell. Off
the main highway. Summer surf.

HAWAIIAN VILLAGE
Two breaks, right and left. South
swell. Off the main highway
near Mil-Lii town.

Cranking into the soup as the thick shoulder flattens.

A smooth face looms ahead as rider jams for the shoulder.

"The Sunset Hook" . . . This photograph captures the feeling of power generated by the big winter surf. Shown here are two traits common to island waves. First, a steep wave face which produces an almost vertical takeoff. Second, a thick, hooking lip which breaks from top-to-bottom over a coral reef. **Note:** Photographer braved fierce currents to capture this unusual angle. (Photo by Wilkings.)

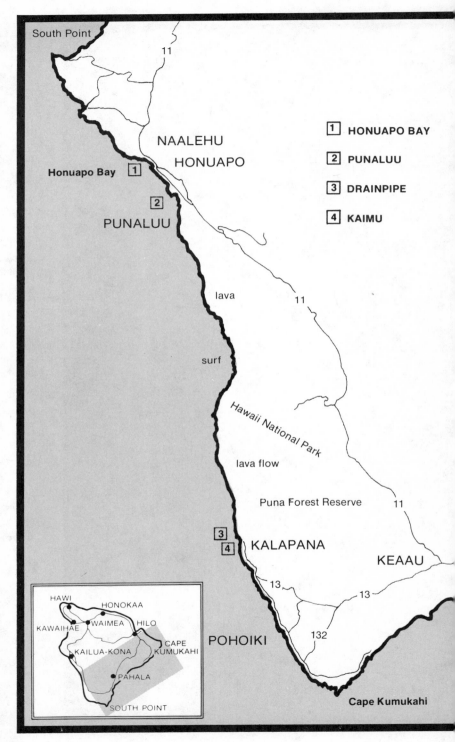

South Point

11

NAALEHU
HONUAPO

Honuapo Bay [1]

[2]

PUNALUU

lava

surf

Hawaii National Park

lava flow

Puna Forest Reserve

11

[3]
[4] KALAPANA

KEAAU

13

13

132

POHOIKI

Cape Kumukahi

[1] HONUAPO BAY

[2] PUNALUU

[3] DRAINPIPE

[4] KAIMU

HAWI   HONOKAA
KAWAIHAE   WAIMEA   HILO
KAILUA-KONA   CAPE
                        KUMUKAHI
        PAHALA
    SOUTH POINT

Shoreline: Access to the surf breaks along this rugged coast is nearly impossible. Miles upon miles of raw lava separate the highway from the sea. Ridable waves can be found in the few places where side roads wend their way to the sea.

Wind: The northeast trades are very unpredictable. They roar along the shoreline creating irregular surface conditions. Mornings and evenings usually produce the cleanest shape.

Swell: South swells produce long, well-defined lines. East and west wind swells generate junky winter surf.

Notes: The reefs are covered with lava, coral and sea urchins — use caution when stepping down.

SURFING AREAS

HONUAPO
Muscular lefts off point. Needs strong south swell to work. Summer juice.

PUNALUU
Short rights over shallow reef. Off main highway. Black sand beach. Year 'round.

DRAINPIPE
Long right slides. Breaks 5-20 feet. Sharp lava beach. Summer and Winter.

KAIMU
A black sand beach. Rights and lefts. Best on south swell, no wind. Breaks year 'round.

Strong tradewinds hold the crest while rider streaks for the shoulder.

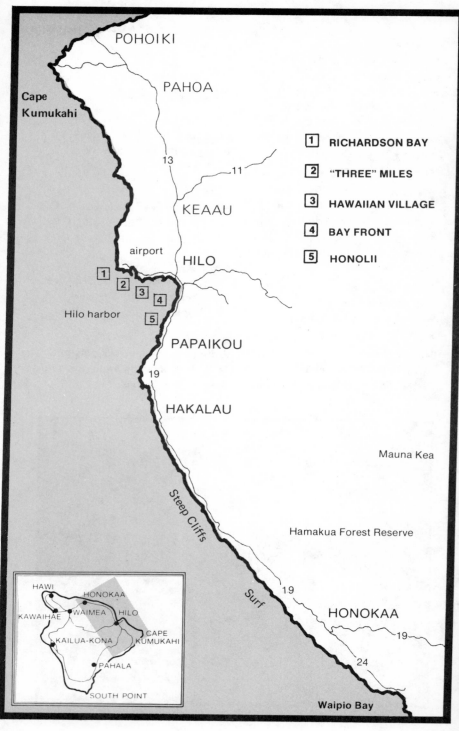

POHOIKI

PAHOA

Cape
Kumukahi

13

11

KEAAU

airport

HILO

1 RICHARDSON BAY

2 "THREE" MILES

3 HAWAIIAN VILLAGE

4 BAY FRONT

5 HONOLII

Hilo harbor

1
2
3
4
5

PAPAIKOU

19

HAKALAU

Mauna Kea

Hamakua Forest Reserve

Steep Cliffs

Surf

19

HONOKAA

19

24

HAWI

HONOKAA

KAWAIHAE

WAIMEA

HILO

KAILUA-KONA

CAPE
KUMUKAHI

PAHALA

SOUTH POINT

Waipio Bay

88

Inside reefs can produce hollow and unexpected sections.

Shoreline: Very little is known of the coastal area between Cape Kumukahi and Hilo Bay. Highway 13 runs far inland isolating many potential surf breaks. . . . Near the city of Hilo, open beaches and coast roads provide easy access to all surfing areas. . . . The rivermouths between Hilo and Waipio Bay produce consistent, well-shaped surf. But vertical lava cliffs make entry to these areas nearly impossible. . . . At Honokaa, a narrow side road leads toward Waipio Valley. Access to this lush valley and uncrowded surf is by foot or jeep only.

Wind: This is Windward Hawaii. The northeast trades blow onshore producing constant choppy conditions. Occasional kona storms create surfable smoothness.

Swell: North and east swells generate strong winter surf. During the summer months, windblown east swells create small, bumpy waves.

Notes: When a huge north swell and kona wind combine, uncrowded perfection will result.

SURFING AREAS

RICHARDSON BAY
Long, powerful rights off point. Needs 8 foot north swell. Mornings and evenings best.

THREE MILES
Right slide off rocky point. 3-8 feet. North or East swell. Variable winds. Winter.

HAWAIIAN VILLAGE
Rugged rights. 4-20 feet. Needs kona wind. Winter break.

BAY FRONT
Mile long rights into Hilo Bay. Needs huge north swell. Kona winds. Winter surf.

HONOLII
Point left, short right slides. Big in winter, small during summer. Rocky bottom. Rivermouth.

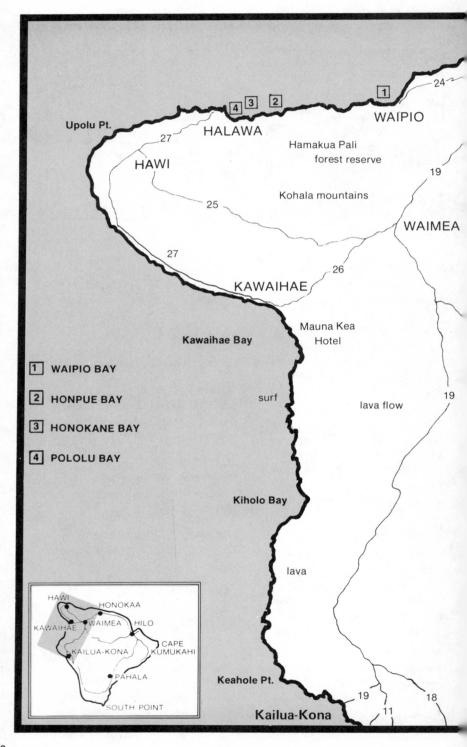

Upolu Pt.

WAIPIO

HALAWA

HAWI

Hamakua Pali
forest reserve

Kohala mountains

WAIMEA

KAWAIHAE

Kawaihae Bay

Mauna Kea
Hotel

surf

lava flow

1 WAIPIO BAY

2 HONPUE BAY

3 HONOKANE BAY

4 POLOLU BAY

Kiholo Bay

lava

Keahole Pt.

Kailua-Kona

HAWI   HONOKAA
KAWAIHAE WAIMEA   HILO
          CAPE
KAILUA-KONA KUMUKAHI
       PAHALA
   SOUTH POINT

24
19
27
25
27
26
19
19
18
11

A cylindrical tube forms overhead — "Pipeline", Oahu.

WAIPIO BAY TO KAWAIHAE

Shoreline: The bays northwest of Waipio produce ridable surf year 'round. Long hikes through lush valleys are required to reach these rarely visited areas. . . . Many potential surf breaks exist between Hawi and Kawaihae but lava, steep cliffs, and private property restrict access.

Wind: Brisk tradewinds blow onshore. Smooth surface conditions can usually be found in the mornings or evenings. Offshore winds prevail during kona storms.

Swell: North and west swells generate powerful winter surf. Summer wind swells produce small, bumpy waves.

Notes: Only the hardiest should attempt hiking into these isolated valleys.

SURFING AREAS

WAIPIO BAY

Various reef breaks, right and left. Access by jeep or horse. Isolated surf year' round.

HONOPUE BAY

Unsurfed, unseen bay. Access by long hike. Tropical paradise. Breaks year 'round.

HONOKANE BAY

Rights and lefts over reef. Rarely surfed. Inaccessible by auto. Breaks Summer and Winter.

POLOLU BAY

Reef breaks, right and left. Lush valley. Access by foot. Unsurfed. Summer and Winter.

KAWAIHAE TO KAILUA-KONA

Shoreline: Numerous small breaks can be found along the white sand beaches of Kawaihae Bay. . . . Very little is known of the coast from Puako to Kailua-Kona. Miles of jagged lava separate the highway from the sea and access is by foot or jeep.

Swell: This area receives surf year 'round. North and west swells produce clean winter walls. Summer south swells generate smaller, softer tubes.

Wind: Ideal tradewinds create perfect shape most of the year. Kona storms quickly destroy glassy conditions.

Notes: Commercial development is underway. A new highway will soon open up this virgin coastline.

Off on the peak as crowd scrambles up the face — "Sunset Beach", Oahu.

A new highway will soon open up virgin coastline along the western shore of Hawaii.

CREDITS

Research and Text — Bank Wright

Articles by — Susan Jessen

Photography by — Steve Wilkings and Peter French

Graphic Design by — Kathy McKeen

Island Maps by — Bill Penaroza

Island Verse by — Warren Vignato

Printed by — The Tivoli Printing Company, Los Angeles, California

ACKNOWLEDGMENTS

Many people have contributed thought, study and encouragement to this guide. It would be impossible to list them all here. I appreciate these generous sacrifices. It is my sincere hope that through this book both surfers and non-surfers become more aware of the beauty of Hawaii's natural environment.

The Author